Education is not the filling of a pail but the lighting of a fire.

WB Yeats

This is a story about Sam.

Sam is 15.

Sam lives with Mum and baby sister.

Sam is funny, kind and clever.

But Sam gets into trouble at school.

Last year, Sam spent six weeks in a Pupil Referral Unit. This summer Sam started smoking skunk. Sam was given it by a boy who is two years older and an elder in a gang that controls the estate. Now Sam's got an eight-inch blade under the mattress. He asked Sam to keep it safe. This isn't what Sam aspires to. But status is a new sensation; and Sam can't see a whole lot of alternative. Sam thinks about quitting education altogether.

A good thing in Sam's life is Jo. Jo's a youth worker. Sam's known Jo for six years, ever since Sam started going to the youth club. Most weekends and holidays, Jo's doing stuff with Sam and other young people who live on the block – running their own community projects, on residential weekends in the Chilterns or adventuring in the Ashdown Forest. Young people talk to Jo. Sam's smart. Sam trusts Jo. On better days Sam finds enough confidence to believe Jo when Jo says Sam could go to university. It's because of Jo's influence, and help navigating the system, that Sam will. It's largely because of what Sam learns with Jo that Sam will become the author of Sam's own story. It's not just because of Jo that this story's going to have a happy ending. (Sam's Mum, a teacher, a nurse, a vicar and an uncle will all play their part.) But Jo's definitely important.

This is also a story about Shafiq.

Shafiq is 19.

Shafiq lives with an Aunt.

Shafiq is lively, aware and charming.

Shafiq has never been in any trouble of note, doing well at school and now starting an apprenticeship.

Shafiq has known AJ for a decade. AJ volunteers at the youth club down Shafiq's road. AJ hasn't rescued Shafiq. But AJ (and others) have helped Shafiq understand how society works and how to lead in a variety of settings – how to influence, communicate and cajole. And Shafiq feels more cheerful and more fulfilled by helping other young people, being respected and knowing he's part of the community.

Shafiq's story isn't all that exciting, truth be told. Or at least, it's not dramatic. Shafiq's never featured in a funding bid or press release. Shafiq's just getting on with it – but better and more rounded because of AJ.

Contents

Foreword

It is now 15 months since we first published *Hunch*, back in November 2011. And while we have not – thankfully – had a repeat of the violent unrest that erupted in the summer of 2011, the prevailing economic difficulties have meant that the challenges facing young people around jobs, education and opportunities have shown few real signs of improvement.

As 2012 closed, we found that we were down to the very last few copies of *Hunch* and considering whether to reprint. Over Christmas, we asked a group of colleagues and friends to re-read it, to see whether any of it needed updating or, with the benefit of a little distance, we wanted to change any of the arguments that had felt so compelling at the time.

We hope it doesn't sound complacent to say that we were all of the view that the narrative we had described, and the case we had set out in *Hunch* – for the importance of good youth work – was emphatically still valid now, over a year after we had first made it.

So this edition is not really new. The words, the ideas and the critique offered are the same as when we first published. But it feels like there is a pressing current need for a restatement of these ideas and arguments.

There are some key questions that affect young people – and have an impact on all of us – which we absolutely believe *Hunch* can help us answer. Questions such as how we harness the spirit of volunteering and social action that became so evident during the Olympics. Or how in the current economic climate we create sustainable opportunities for young people and equip those young people to take them.

We believe that good youth work – which gives young people the opportunity to learn and to have fun, in safe, informal settings (and not just in the boundaries of a youth club building), under the guidance of a trusted, independent adult – can and must help us answer these questions.

In the same way it can help us confront the challenge of the small but still worrying number of young people who persist in settling arguments and disputes with violence, and the more fundamental questions about how we give young people a genuine stake in their own communities, and then help them grow beyond them.

Walking through Upper Clapton in Hackney last month we asked directions to Springfield Youth Club, one of our member clubs, which is run entirely by local volunteers. Three teenagers volunteered to escort us there. They told us how the youth workers at the club have the status of local heroes. And that Springfield is somewhere they had chosen to go throughout their teenage years, where they haven't been judged for not excelling at Maths or English – and where they developed their confidence and skills. In a community riddled with gangs, Springfield has made them positive local role models. Two of them are now qualified sports coaches and one is at college.

If ever we needed a reminder of the value of the positive impact of youth work, there it was. And if ever anyone could sum up the arguments in *Hunch* in a way that everybody could understand, then it was those three teenage boys in Clapton.

We want all young Londoners to have the best of this incredible capital city; for it to invest in their potential, encourage them as leaders in their communities and open up opportunities for them to thrive.

If it's your first time, we hope you enjoy reading *Hunch*. And if you are returning to it, we hope it means as much to you the second time around.

Prologue

How do young people become good adults?

The question might feel particularly pertinent after the events of this summer. But the spur to this short essay is found not in August 2011 but two years earlier. Between May 2009 and March 2011, London Youth ran Positive Change, a programme targeting young people in or at risk of joining criminal gangs.

Positive Change was a success.[1] Far from being a panacea, the programme nonetheless proved to be a valuable way of preventing anti-social behaviour and youth violence. It was also effective at providing exit routes for those already involved in gang culture.

As such, we (London Youth) determined to write up what we had learnt. Initially we thought we would write a very short manual – an aide memoire for practitioners and policy makers, focused on youth violence. Certainly, specific goals were achieved and particular lessons learnt, and we have published these (together with a full literature review and short case-studies) on our website.

However, as we began to unpack what had worked (and why), what we'd do (and not do) again, the deconstruction of Positive Change did not so much unearth new knowledge about how to tackle a particular problem (in this case preventing crime and gang association) as highlight the fundamental importance of developing young people's social knowledge and networks, their all-round capabilities and character.

---

1. Nearly 2,000 young people were engaged in a wide range of interventions. To drill down into just one aspect of a hydra-headed initiative, we worked with 112 young people in HM Young Offenders' Institution Portland about how to return to their communities in London, combining cognitive behavioural therapy in group settings pre-release with through-the-gate support into education and employment: of 56 who have been released so far, 12 have re-offended: a recidivism rate of 21% versus a Youth Justice Board annualised norm of 74%.

Positive Change demonstrated the value of access to adults with the commitment and skills to give independent support and advice to help show how society works and navigate the transition to adulthood. It showed that young people need the opportunity to come together and learn outside the classroom, find the things they're good at and be part of something positive in order to develop personal qualities and social competence.

These are simple truths, a benefit to us all and an integral part of a well-functioning society. They are an important way of meeting core policy objectives (including increasing employability and reducing criminality). They are also critical means of building strong communities and national well-being more broadly.

Much of such support will be provided informally (by extended family or friends). It might also be achieved through wider services for young people (including school or vocational training) or as a by-product of a different relationship (with a teacher, sports coach or preacher). It can also be created deliberately by youth work.

And everyone has a part to play: in families, schools and communities; as youth workers; as parents, friends and neighbours; as employers and colleagues; as opinion-formers, funders and policy makers – in all our many roles, as we help young people become good adults.

We want to be clear that we didn't start writing in August 2011. Yet, inescapably, what happened that summer has shone a light on the question of how young people can be cherished and challenged to be the best they can be.

Introduction

Capabilities, qualities, competencies or character. Whichever term we prefer, there is a remarkable degree of consensus that the making of a good life lies not only in our formal skills and knowledge but equally in our wider abilities, ambition and attitude.[2] And if such foundations cannot necessarily be taught, evidence and experience certainly show they can be developed.

Yet in the oceans of ink and days of debate on young people, though we read much about formal education (about schools and vocational training) and hear plenty about particular problems (such as youth violence, or unemployment), we see relatively little reference to the development of young people's underlying capabilities. Discourse is largely silent on the more fundamental (and optimistic) question of how we develop good and effective citizens. As such, beyond the youth sector itself, popular and political debate consistently overlook the notion of youth work, of broad-based personal and social development, and what it can achieve.

It was not always thus. Speak to men and women born before 1950 and, typically, you find ready acknowledgement that young people grow up in schools and families and communities – and a corresponding sense that the informal education of healthy role models and structured fun is a critical bridge between the perils of adolescence and a successful adult life. Yet such self and societal awareness appears to have waned – at least explicitly.

Implicitly, most of us can think back to a point in our teen years when we learnt something profound about ourselves and the world – a critical point of insight of life-long value. And for most of us this point of reference will recall a time outside

2. There is no definitive categorisation of core capabilities though there are common clusters including: personal qualities such as empathy, confidence, resilience and self-control; non formal skills including creativity, problem-solving, agency (the ability to act independently) and communication; and social knowledge including networks and the ability to build alliances, negotiate authority and work within systems.

of the classroom, involve a sensible adult who was not our parent and include peers. Yet, bluntly, human truth does not seem to be surviving translation from personal experience to contemporary debate.

Our point is this: we fear the simplicity of youth work – the essential proposition that young people benefit from trusting relationships with reliable adults, a positive peer group and the chance to learn from a range of new opportunities – has fallen from fashion at precisely the time we need it most. Shouldn't investment in all-round capabilities – as opposed to tackling presenting problems in isolation – form the keystone of public interest and policy? We have a hunch that it should.

- So this short essay attempts to reclaim an idea.

- We argue there is a pressing need to prioritise character, champion the virtue of a rounded education and re-discover the value of good youth work.

- Our aim is to begin conversations.

We hope that what follows will be of interest to youth workers, others who work, fund and volunteer with young people, and the interested citizen alike. For the very-rushed, we include a two-page summary at the end. Otherwise, you'll find four short sections unpacking:

1. What we mean by good youth work

2. How we know good youth work works

3. Why youth work got forgotten; and, crucially,

4. What is to be done?

For our purpose is not to defend but explore. Nor, whilst wholly cognisant of the cuts, is it a plaintive cry for the tap to be turned back on, so much as an idea of how adolescence might best be supported when the economy comes back: what's next is what matters.

1. What we mean by good youth work

The perils and simplicity of a definition

Eddie George, former Governor of the Bank of England, once observed there are three sorts of economist: those who can add up, and those who can't. There are at least 1,372 sorts of youth worker.

Or, in other words, whilst there is general agreement that youth work is, 'the process by which we learn from our experiences and become more effective in our decisions and in our relationships',[3] thereafter the glass darkens.

Clearly, the fact youth work means subtly different things to different people is inimical to building a trusted brand.

Worse, as well as confusing, it is also a bind: on one hand, if we cannot make a clear definition, we can scarcely advance an idea; on the other, if we narrow the definition too far, we create a priesthood in which only qualified professionals pursuing pre-approved techniques can practice. Furthermore, attempts at definition inevitably invite endless debates about the 'precise meaning' or 'true nature' of a thing, arguably retarding practical advance.

We take a broad view: good youth work promotes personal and social development.

When we use the term 'youth work', we are referring to a wide range of work with young people that develops the rounded individual and typically includes learning from:

- a responsible adult

- a positive peer group

- a range of activities

3. Personal Development Point – www.personaldevelopmentpoint.com

- taking responsibility

- being part of something communal and positive

As such, youth work (or a youth work approach) can be undertaken by specialist youth work organisations; as an integral aspect of other activities young people take part in (such as arts or sports); within wider services for young people (including schools); and in services and walks of life that young people also experience (including the work place).

A youth work approach can be applied wherever young people learn of life. And this, we suggest, is a crucial point. Not only might public policy valuably refresh and renew a commitment to youth work in its deliberate form, as practised by specialist youth workers; we can also helpfully explore how the principles of youth work can inform public life more broadly. What can youth work mean for schools, public services, family support and communities?

Evidence and experience suggest, overwhelmingly, that every young person, irrespective of background and circumstance, has something to gain from somewhere to go, something to do and someone to talk to. And it is in the combination of role model and mentor, good friends, structured fun and informal education that the genius of good youth work resides.[4]

So our conviction is that whilst the prosecution of good youth work is as complex as human individuality demands, the idea of good youth work is intuitive and straightforward.

---

4. For example, a 2003 study of more than 600 programmes in Australia concluded that the long-term impact of constructive activities can only be accomplished in combination with supporting young people to improve their personal and social skills and change their behaviour – Morris et al. (2003)

Characteristics of good youth work

In a little more detail, we suggest, 'good' youth work is also...

Focused on people not problems

Good youth work pays attention to an individual's particular needs and personality. It does not address isolated skills, nor tackle presenting deficits, so much as develop the whole young person. For example, a critical success factor for Positive Change related to a youth worker's ability to build relationships with individuals as individuals, not on the basis of their gang status. Equally, we see that youth work can benefit all young people. Everybody gains from sensible adult influences beyond parental concern, a positive peer group and the chance to try and succeed at new things. Youth work is not solely for those 'in need' or disadvantaged.

Facilitating personal and social development

Good youth work is about informal education. Simply providing activities is baby-sitting for teenagers. Good youth clubs are places of reflection and debate, challenge and creativity. They provide opportunities to learn and practice personal and social skills (plus, in many instances, supplementary formal education). If they do not, they are simply bad leisure centres.

About taking responsibility

Good youth clubs are places where young people are supported to take responsibility and assume leadership. Co-production is never more relevant than in a good youth club. Supporting young people to be involved in how things run is central to their purpose. This isn't necessarily about formal advisory and governance structures (though that helps too) but about a culture of incremental opportunities for taking responsibility. At its best, an under-13s football team doesn't just turn up on a Saturday morning and play. Each member has their own responsibility: kit, pick-up times, match fixtures, refreshments and referees. And they generally don't let each other down. By the time they are 17, two of the team are qualified sports coaches training the club's next generation. Good youth work does not simply provide services; it helps young people establish a sense of contribution and narrative, a sense of belonging and purpose.

About developing agency

Agency is the ability to act independently within society, to be the author of your own life story. It is increasingly important as transitions to adulthood become more varied and complex. Good youth work increases agency by developing capabilities and character. It also develops social knowledge: good youth work raises aspirations and develops the savvy to help achieve them, providing independent advice and perspective to help young people navigate social systems and networks.

Chosen by young people

Good youth work works, in part, because young people choose to be involved.[5]

Especially strong when locally-led and trusted...

We do not privilege one particular form of youth work over another: all can point to evidence of having a positive impact on confidence, life-skills and motivation. Many young people benefit from personal and social development programmes without ever having crossed the threshold of a youth club. Equally, and particularly for those growing up in the most deprived areas, the youth club may be one of the few opportunities available to them, outside of school and family, to develop core personal and social skills.[6] The principle of open access, allied to local leadership and a youth club's ability to build trust, provides a sense of security and ownership. Working, sharing and learning across generations with families and communities, as well as young people, is also highly valuable.

---

5. Clearly, choice in this sense exists on a spectrum from spontaneous self-selection (albeit propelled by underpinning antecedents such as having knowledge of the service's existence and the confidence to self-select) to voluntary engagement following dedicated outreach targeted towards the most disengaged. Yet, even in HMYOI Portland young people chose to take part in Positive Change with no element of compulsion. The vast majority of participants self-referred and attendance was over 95%.

6. Sorhaindo and Feinstein (2007); New Local Government Network (2008)

... and developed over the long-term.

We absolutely do not disregard the role that short, sharp shocks (so to speak) can play in young people's development. Indeed, the evidence from Positive Change (and scores of other interventions) is that personal trust and example can be forged with relative speed by a skilled practitioner. Equally, the long-term development of relationships can be especially powerful, providing vital stability in potentially chaotic lives. As the inspirational and influential academic-turned-community-worker, Bob Holman has put it, it is much harder (albeit not impossible) aged 16 to disregard the influence of (or pull a knife on) the person who has taken you swimming since the age of five than it is to ignore the peripatetic project worker bussed in for a six-week scheme. (And the relationship is ever-stronger, if that youth worker also takes your brother away on an annual camping trip and is helping your little cousin with her homework.)

Structured

Good youth work is structured. Indeed, birth cohort studies indicate that youth clubs providing completely unstructured activities do little or nothing to develop young people.[7]

However, by structured we do not mean regimented. By structured we mean purposeful.

Often, the initial attraction for engaging young people might be the lure of a particular activity.

There is also a place for non-structured down-time: purposeful activity is important, and so, sometimes, is sitting on the step and making friends and having fun and building trust.

Further, purposefulness can be found in activities that may seem, at first glance, unstructured. A group outing to Alton Towers, for example, might involve young people organising

7. Feinstein et al. (2005); Mahoney et al. (2004)

the trip, or running the day for younger young people, taking a degree of responsibility for the care of their juniors.

Meanwhile, screaming along on the roller coaster, the youth worker might informally be building trust. Relationships sit at the heart of good youth work. And a conversation in the mini-bus on the way back might be the moment that a young person confides in their youth worker about what is really going on at home.

Skillfully facilitated

Good youth work is highly skilled.

So we are clear about the need for investment in the skills and personal development of those who practise it. We are equally cautious as to the risk of over-professionalisation. For good youth work sees two different skill-sets at play:

1. Interpersonal skills – the character and social competence of the youth worker

2. Technical skills and knowledge – depending on the context and method of youth work

Certainly, young people are quick to spot the shallow and the glib and want and need sources of knowledge and expertise. For example, young people involved in Positive Change are clear that their youth workers needed to understand the systems of formal and alternative education and criminal justice in order to proffer good advice. Or, in outdoor education or sports development, the technical skill of the instructor is essential – for safety, credibility and to ensure that personal and social development is interwoven within activity.

But good youth workers also need the emotional and social intelligence to listen, cajole, manage conflict and inspire leadership in others. And even though experience, formal training and peer-group reflection can all combine to increase effectiveness, this skill-set is by no means limited to the professional youth worker.

For example, in the spring of 2011, thanks to The Co-Sponsorship Agency and v, we teamed up with Wickes, Pimlico Plumbers and Streatham Youth and Community Trust to pilot a programme called Volunteer It Yourself. 45 young people came together with professional tradespeople to do up the local youth club.

The great strength of the programme was not 'just' volunteers going into a place to help do it up, but skilled tradespeople sharing knowledge of their skills on a real job that was equally the responsibility of youth club members. And we would argue strongly that the relationships developed between the young people and their 'skills mentors' did much by way of teaching invaluable life lessons related to professional pride, punctuality and the line between banter and rudeness. None was a professional, or even conscious youth worker, yet good youth work was clearly at play.

A taxonomy of good youth work

Our argument is that youth work is a broad and straightforward idea. As such, youth work comes in subtly different guises, comprising a range of specific objectives, forms and styles.

Aims

Broadly, youth work is the positive promotion of personal and social development.[8]

The National Occupational Standards for Youth Work describes its objectives as enabling young people to develop holistically; working with them to facilitate their personal, social and educational development; enabling them to develop their voice, influence and place in society; supporting them to reach their full potential; and helping to remove barriers to young people's development and to achieve positive outcomes and a successful transition to adult life.[9]

At London Youth we talk about helping young people be the best they can be.

Emerging work from The Young Foundation, National Youth Agency and Local Government Association helpfully unpacks this broad aim further, highlighting the existence of both intrinsic and extrinsic outcomes.

Intrinsic outcomes are relevant to the well-being of the individual, of value in and of themselves (including happiness, friendship and resilience).

Extrinsic outcomes are directly relevant to the wider social good. They are more readily quantifiable (such as increased employment, reduced crime, and community cohesion).

---

8. Oginsky (2010)
9. Children's Workforce Development Council (2010)

This distinction is similar but not identical to the common differentiation between 'soft' and 'hard' outcomes. We see it as helpful because it suggests a continuum, and implied causal relationship, between underlying capabilities and specific attainment.

Intrinsic Outcomes
Such as:
- Happiness
- Friendships
- Confidence
- Resilience

Extrinsic Outcomes
Such as:
- Increased Employment
- Reduced Crime
- Community Cohesion

Another helpful distinction is between 'risk' factors (such as family conflict or exposure to weapons and drugs) related to an individual developing 'problem behaviours' (such as youth violence); and 'protective' factors (such as a pro-social peer group or a resilient temperament) which reduce these chances.[10]

Although much recent practice has focused on the targeted reduction of risk factors, the extent to which risk factors correlate with or are causal to later problems remains under debate. Nor do we know clearly the relative weighting of certain risk factors. On the other hand, research from the increasingly influential Positive Youth Development movement in the USA shows how investing in interventions which increase protective factors are as valuable as, if not more than, projects targeting particular risk factors,[11] suggesting the value of broad-based personal and social development alongside problem-focused interventions.

---

10. Hawkins et al. (2000); Arthur et al. (2002)
11. Lerner et al. (2009)

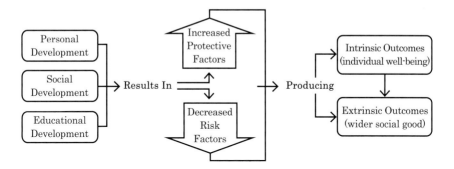

Means

We suggest later in this essay that one of the reasons youth work has been forgotten beyond its own immediate sector is because subtly different practitioners have failed to rally under one broad banner. We also note that, almost certainly out of frustration with the diminishing youth work brand, practitioners have at times defined themselves by a subset of youth work (such as outreach or mentoring), robbing the core idea of some of its best examples.

As such, it seems sensible to acknowledge that approaches to youth work vary across four key axes.[12]

Including groupings by:
- Age
- Gender*
- Geography
- Sexual Orientation
- Ethnicity
- Faith
- Disability

Including:
- Self and Peer Referral
- Membership
- Outreach
- Targeted Support
- Drop-In

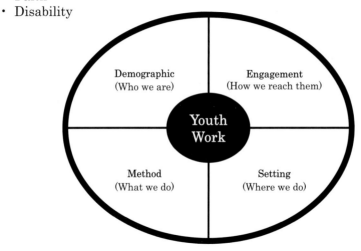

Including groupings by:
- Sports
- Arts
- Music
- Mentoring and Coaching
- Key-working or Group Work
- Youth Action and Leadership

Including:
- Club-based
- Public Spaces
- Residential Centres
- The Outdoors

---

12. Particular thanks to Bryan Merton for this analysis.

* Key learning from Positive Change and from Race on the Agenda's report on *The Female Voice in Violence* suggests a particularly pressing need to re-invest in working specifically with girls and young women – www.rota.org.uk/pages/FVV.aspx

Similarly, the principle that youth work is focused on young people's wider learning is reflected in the fact youth work can be found in forms of intervention variable by the degree and nature of their design.[13]

Guided Reflection

Reactive Learning
Young people assess their beliefs, values and options and make more effective life choices with the assistance of skilled staff

Programmatic Learning
Provision is a focused programme of selected activities and guided reflection designed to achieve a particular outcome or outcomes

Unplanned ———————|——————— **Planned**

Independent Learning
Provision is an environment which is conducive to learning; for example a play area, a creative area, a quiet room or a youth centre

Activity – Based Learning
Provision is activity based; for example games, team building, volunteering opportunities, sports, problem solving, debates

Self-Reflection

---

13. Thanks to Paul Oginsky for this model.

It is also important to recognise that the principles of youth work can be undertaken both by specialist organisations and in other spheres of life – hence our emphasis on youth work and the youth work approach.

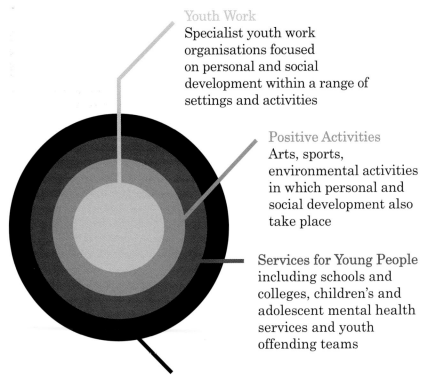

Youth Work
Specialist youth work organisations focused on personal and social development within a range of settings and activities

Positive Activities
Arts, sports, environmental activities in which personal and social development also take place

Services for Young People including schools and colleges, children's and adolescent mental health services and youth offending teams

Services Young People Access
such as the NHS and Job Centre Plus

2. How we know good youth work works

This section comes in two parts. The first makes clear the limits of our claim and knowledge. The second spells out how we can have confidence that good youth work works.

The limits of our claim and knowledge

As with any enthusiast, there is a risk of our saying 'youth work is the answer, what is the question?'

There is plentiful evidence that good youth work begets a wide range of positive outcomes. Equally, it is arguable that broad assertion has been a historic flaw in youth work's own narrative.

Youth work is not a panacea

Clearly, influences on young people are multiple. Pinpointing the effect of good youth work is extremely difficult. A 2000 study for the US Department of Justice explored influences on adolescence through consideration of five domains – individual, familial, school, peer and community – and such seems a sensible starting point.[14]

Parents and families are the most significant influence (for good or ill) in the lives of almost all young people. Cohort studies make clear that family size, parental affirmation or condemnation, inter-parental and family stability, parental education, and employment can impact greatly on educational attainment, offending and employment.[15] British children's educational attainment and broader life chances remain overwhelmingly linked to parental occupation, income, and qualifications.[16]

Of course, school matters and is absolutely fundamental to child and adolescent development, helping to address educational, physical and emotional needs.[17] At no point is it our intention

---

14. Hawkins et al. (2000)
15. Shader (2002)
16. Lupton (2009); Sodha and Margo (2010)

to set youth work and schools, informal and formal education against one another. Clearly, young people need both.

Research is equally clear that a range of community factors put young people at risk – including poverty, neighbourhood disorganisation, poor housing, crime and violence, and the availability of drugs and guns.[18]

Indeed, Beveridge's five Giant Evils (squalor, ignorance, want, idleness and disease)[19] sound dated and almost certainly hold true: obviously, life chances depend on housing, education, poverty, employment and health.

In short, young people grow up in a political, economic and social landscape far beyond the immediate sphere of influence of a local youth club or brilliant youth worker. As Sam's short story sets out, nobody forgets a great youth worker – and there are no magic answers.

There are limits to the evidence base

Whilst a great and increasing amount of data on young people has been collected in the past decade, (largely in the form of programme management information) it is not collected in one place, it is of different forms and it is usually collected locally because services are locally delivered.

1958 and 1970 birth cohort studies excepted, there is a lack of longitudinal research.[20]

In most instances, the sample size is small.

---

17. Centre for Analysis of Social Exclusion (2011); Flannery (1997); Furlong and Morrison (2000); Reynolds et al. (1996); Thomas and Mortimore (1996)
18. Hawkins et al. (2000); Calhoun (2001); Loeber and Farrington (2000); Pitts (2008)
19. Beveridge (1942)
20. Feinstein et al. (2005)

And despite increasing interest in the assessment of long-term impact and value for money,[21] there are few examples of studies that succeed in quantifying and comparing the costs and benefits of individual programmes. (The exception is Merton et al.'s Evaluation of the impact of youth work in England in 2004.) [22]

These facts considered, next to clinical medicine, for example, our science comes up, relatively short.

However...

... the cumulative effect of evaluations of individual programmes,

- set alongside the consistent experience of practitioners and young people

- supplemented by survey data

- to say nothing of powerful anecdotal evidence...

...does yield rich seams of insight.

It is not true that youth work has no evidence.

There are limitations to the evidence base.

There is a strong sense of direction - that should pass the test of any reasonable person.

Therefore, immediately below, we summarise a selection of evidence, in order to demonstrate the efficacy of youth work related to:

- educational attainment and employment

- crime

- character and the wider capabilities necessary for a successful life

---

21. Feinstein et al. (2005)
22. See for example social return on investment and social audit.

The value of good youth work

Increasing formal education attainment and employability

- In the UK, more than one in ten children leave school with no qualifications[23]

- During the academic year 2009-10, an estimated 5,740 young people were permanently excluded from schools across England[24]

- There were 991,000 unemployed 16 to 24 year olds in the three months to August 2011[25]

- 57% of employers are unhappy with young people's self-management skills[26]

What role is there here for good youth work?

It is certainly evidenced that personal and social development, the kernel of good youth work, underpins formal educational attainment and employability. For example, Social and Emotional Aspects of Learning (SEAL), currently taken up by 60% of UK primary schools and 15% of secondary schools, consistently reap success: of 17 international SEAL programmes assessed, all had notably reduced aggression, depression, impulsiveness and anti-social behaviour, and developed cooperation, resilience, optimism, empathy and a positive and realistic self-concept.[27]

Emphatically, our argument is not to set youth work and schools in competition. Quite the opposite. Yet, we know that good schools alone are not enough. Young people in Britain spend less than 15% of their waking hours in formal education.[28]

---

23. Centre for Social Justice (2007)
24. Centre for Social Justice (2011)
25. Office for National Statistics (October 2011)
26. CBI (2010)
27. Wells et al. (2003)
28. House of Commons Education Committee (2011)

And schools are subject to understandable pressure to succeed in exam results, inevitably focusing them on formal, cognitive skills (and, many teachers complain, 'teaching to the test').

Yet we know that educational attainment depends as much on non-cognitive as cognitive skills.[29] Self-discipline, for example, is more than twice as important as IQ in predicting academic results.[30] Consistent and recurring participation in extra-curricular activities can promote educational attainment and lower rates of school dropout, whilst boosting interpersonal competence and personal aspiration.[31] Indeed, the *Examination of the Longitudinal Study of Young People in England* (LSYPE) reveals that those who engage in structured developmental activities achieve 10-20% higher GCSE scores.[32] Youth work has also been shown to heighten motivation for learning and self-efficacy[33] and to be an effective aid to overcoming educational barriers linked to socio-economic disadvantage.[34]

Youth work is also a proven developer of key employability skills (as defined by the 2010 UK Commission for Employment and Skills).[35] For example, in the spring of 2011, Professor Alison Wolf's *Review of Vocational Education* confirmed that the experience of work and the capabilities it develops continues to be valued and rewarded by employers as much as formal credentials. 70% of employers want to see a development of employability skills (including team work and problem solving) made a top priority.[36]

---

29. Non-cognitive skills include initiative-taking, teamwork, problem-solving, emotional management, self-regulation and resilience.

30. Duckworth and Seligman (2005)

31. Mahoney and Cairns (1997); Barber et al. (2001); Mahoney et al. (2004)

32. Cebulla and Tomaszewski (2009)

33. Mahoney et al. (2005)

34. Almlund et al. (2011); Larson et al. (2004)

35. UK Commission for Employment and Skills (March 2010); Hansen et al. (2003); Larson et al. (2004)

36. CBI Education and Skills Survey (2011)

Tackling youth crime and anti-social behaviour

Wary of moral panic, contagious indignation and claims of a crisis of youth, it is nonetheless true that some things are badly wrong.

- When the British Crime Survey asks about local problems, 'teenagers hanging around' is the top response.

- When Her Majesty's Inspector of Constabularies sampled 5,699 people who had called the police in September 2009, 30% cited drunken behaviour and under-age drinking, and 29% cited youths loitering in numbers on the street, as the cause for their concern.

Irrespective of whether such concerns about young people are the product of reason or stigma, significant swathes of the citizenry are afraid of young people's behaviour. And anti-social behaviour and crime are intimately linked: 77% of young people frequently committing an act of anti-social behaviour are also committing a criminal offence.[37]

- In 2007, The Metropolitan Police Service identified 171 youth gangs responsible for more than 40 murders and 20% of the capital's youth crime[38]

- The number of 14-17 year olds imprisoned in England and Wales has doubled since 1990[39]

- Of all European countries excepting Turkey, England and Wales have the highest number of young people in custody[40]

- It costs £60,000 a year to keep a teenager in a young offenders' institution; £215,000 in a secure children's home; and £160,000 in a secure training centre[41]

---

37. Home Office (November 2005); IPPR (2008)
38. Metropolitan Police Service (2007); Local Government Improvement and Development (2008)
39. Independent Commission on Youth Crime and Anti-Social Behaviour (2010)
40. Ibid.
41. Hansard HC, 15 October 2009, c1018W

- We spend 11 times more locking young people up than we do preventing youth crime in the first place[42]

- 74% of young people leaving custody in 2008 re-offended within a year[43]

So what claim can youth work make as a countervailing force for good?

First, key risk factors for anti-social behaviour and offending include association with anti-social peers and a lack of participation in purposeful activities[44] – factors put right by two of the three core facets of good youth work.

Positively, protective factors include meaningful participation in constructive activities.[45] For example, The Audit Commission's 1996 report *Misspent Youth* was clear in recognising the importance of youth work tackling offending and encouraging both the social and emotional development of young participants and pro-social peer relationships.

Likewise, seven out of ten young people think teenagers are involved in anti-social behaviour because they are tired of hanging around. The top priority of low-income parents to enable their children to overcome disadvantage is to find more facilities and activities.[46] And gang members believe, having a significant, respected adult they could turn to is a key factor in preventing criminality.[47]

42. IPPR (2008)
43. Ministry of Justice (2010)
44. Moffitt (1993); Thornberry (1996); Framer and Cadwallader (2000); IPPR (2006)
45. Bernard (1995); Shader (2002)
46. 4Children (2007); Centre for Analysis of Social Exclusion (2011)
47. Korem (1995); Youth Justice Board (2007)

There is certainly no shortage of research connecting good youth work with a reduction in violence and anti-social behaviour. *Dying to Belong*, a 2009 study of violent and criminal gangs by The Centre for Social Justice; Professor John Pitts's 2007 study of youth gangs in Waltham Forest, *Reluctant Gangsters*; and Louise Casey's 2008 review for The Cabinet Office, all highlight the value of skilful youth work diverting young people away from anti-social behaviour and crime.

So too is the broad youth work approach (implicitly) finding currency in an emerging cross-party consensus. The Ministry of Justice's 2010 Green Paper stresses the need to find more effective ways of preventing and reducing youth crime, reserving imprisonment for those who have committed serious offences.[48] Integrated Offender Management (coordinating joint working between different agencies and enabling a holistic approach to be taken to ex-offenders' educational and personal development) and the Youth Justice Pathfinder (driving investment into prevention) further point to increasing awareness of the role of youth work approaches to prevention and rehabilitation.

Building character and capabilities

Yet if good youth work is of demonstrable value to two of the most pressing contemporary social policy goals (increased employability and decreasing crime and violence), it is also of clear intrinsic value to life-long personal and public good.

Whether we prefer the terms, character, capabilities, competencies, personal and social abilities, non-cognitive skills, or (as our grandparents might have had it) 'moral fibre' it is no exaggeration to say that the importance of developing rounded individuals has been established, by philosophers, economists and scientists, beyond all reasonable debate.[49]

---

48. Ministry of Justice (December 2010)
49. For detailed discussion on and evidence for the importance of character, capabilities and non-cognitive skills see especially IPPR (2006); Young Foundation (2009); and Demos (2011).

In classical philosophy, as far back as Plato, the importance of character is seen as inescapable in building communities, 'arête', or virtue, forming the cornerstone of the good republic.

From economics, at least three Nobel laureates make the case. Amartya Sen's work (with Martha Nussbaum) on capabilities demonstrates the importance of the underlying capacity individuals require to succeed. Elinor Ostrom highlights the importance of trust, team-work and cooperation. James Heckman establishes the importance of non-cognitive skills to a wide-range of outcomes (from employment to substance abuse) and cites the five essential OCEAN traits: openness, conscientiousness, extrovertness, agreeableness and neuroticism (meaning attention to detail).[50]

Recent and ground-breaking research in evolutionary biology, neuroscience and genetics yield new insights into the formation and critical importance of such traits as resilience, responsibility and warmth. Developmental psychopathologist, Professor Simon Baron Cohen's work on why some people go down the wrong path focuses on the 'malignant effect of empathy erosion'. The emerging field of positive psychology posits, via the work of Dr. Martin Seligman, five key elements of human flourishing (positive emotions, engagement, relationships, meaning and accomplishment);[51] from Dr. Carol Ryff, six core elements of psychological well-being (autonomy, environmental mastery, personal growth, positive relations with others, purpose in life and self-acceptance);[52] and, from Lord Richard Layard, Geoff Mulgan and Anthony Seldon, ten keys to happiness (giving, relating, exercising, appreciating, trying out, direction, resilience, emotion, acceptance and meaning).[53]

50. Almlund et al. (2011)
51. Forgeard et al. (2011)
52. Ryff and Singer (2008)
53. Action for Happiness – http://www.actionforhappiness.org

Not only do capabilities matter; they matter more and more. Between those born in 1958 and those born in 1970, social and emotional skills became 25% more important in explaining differences in earnings; whilst differences in functional skills became 20% less important.[54]

The Institute for Public Policy Research's (IPPR) 2006 analysis of the changing world in which young people reach adulthood sets out how; whereas pathways from compulsory education to the workplace and 'adult society' were, until the mid 1970s, relatively straightforward and homogenous, now successful transition depends far more on the ability of young people to plan and navigate their own path.[55] Increasing income differentials, the shift to a service economy, more open routes through education and into employment, together with the emphasis of choice in public services and prevailing culture all combine to render personal choice more possible, expected and necessary, thus dramatically raising the importance of individual agency.

In short, capabilities and character count – and increasingly so.

And good youth work increases capability. Two-thirds of young people surveyed in 2004 said youth work had made a considerable difference to their lives, including: increasing confidence; making new friends; learning new skills; making decisions for themselves; and feeling more able to ask for help and information when needed.[56] The 16,000 young people interviewed as part of 4Children's *Youth Review* in 2007 clearly articulated the value of somewhere to go, something to do and someone to talk to.[57] A year earlier, the 19,000 young people consulted in the *Youth Matters* survey emphasised the importance of having places where they felt safe, could call their own, socialise with peers, find supportive adults and access a variety of activities.

---

54. Feinstein (2000)
55. IPPR (2006)
56. Merton et al. (2004)
57. 4Children (2007)

Evidence also links core characteristics of good youth work to the development of core competencies. For example, research underlines the importance of non-parental adults in adolescent development: young people with access to a trusted mentor figure are less likely to participate in high-risk behaviours such as substance misuse and weapon carrying;[58] more resilient than their non-mentored peers;[59] and can exhibit improved attitudinal, behavioural, interpersonal and motivational outcomes.[60]

Evidence further highlights the impact of environment and positive peer groups on character formation. Heckman, for example, demonstrates how peer interaction and relationships are fundamental to the development of non-cognitive skills[61] whilst the influence of peer pressure (for good and ill) is well-established.[62]

Participation in structured activities of the kind associated with good youth work has also been associated with a range of positive outcomes pertaining to the development of character and capabilities.

The Michigan Study of Life Transitions examined 900 participants and found that taking part in pro-social activity in a peer group predicted higher self-esteem and a decrease in loneliness, depressed mood and anxiety.[63]

A comparison of youth-driven and adult-driven youth programmes in the US explored in-depth qualitative data obtained over a three-to four-month cycle of activities. It found that 'youth-driven' activities led to a clear sense of ownership and empowerment and, in turn, improved leadership and planning skills.[64] Structured programmes of athletics and the arts have also been associated with heightened levels of engagement, challenge, enjoyment, motivation and initiative.[65]

---

58. Beier et al. (2000)
59. Southwick et al. (2007)
60. Eby et al. (2008)
61. Heckman (2000)
62. Cialdini (2007); Earls (2009)
63. Barber et al. (2001)
64. Larson et al. (2005)
65. Mahoney et al. (2005)

In their review of theoretical and empirical advances on adolescent development in interpersonal and societal contexts, Smetana et al. suggest involvement in community organisations and service influences the development of greater compassion and interdependence, as well as civic or moral identity and pro-social activity. Civic engagement in adolescence is seen as an important pathway for future citizenship.[66]

Drawing on qualitative longitudinal research, *Positive Development in a Disorderly World* compares emotional and motivational development in various settings, including within the classroom and during free time with friends, and concludes youth work-type programmes are the most supportive for the development of social and emotional intelligence.[67]

And extended anecdotal evidence abounds. For example, in Holman's study, *Kids at the Door Revisited*, the 51 former youth club members that were interviewed all said youth work had offered them: leisure activities which they otherwise would have missed; the opportunity to develop friendships; and the chance to form relationships with adults they trusted. Several believed that the influence, beliefs and practices they learned remained with them throughout adulthood.

We further argue, strongly, that there is an intuitive value to good youth work.

In addition to the weight of scientific enquiry, we know good youth work works because we see it – in the streets and lives of the young people we work with every day.

Yet we are not alone in our conviction.

66. Smetana et al. (2006)
67. Larson (2011)

In our observation, private individuals with (a) children; and (b) disposable cash, invariably purchase progressively higher-value youth work. The beginning may be the petrol or bus fare to take part in a Saturday sports or arts club. Next comes a summer camp or supplementary schooling. At the 'upper' end, the very wealthy have historically outsourced adolescent angst altogether via the British boarding school system. (We appreciate this is a slightly odd way to make the point. And please read this footnote if you think we are simply singing a hymn to the public schools.)[68]

Too often, youth work has to struggle furiously to make its case for creating opportunities for young people from poorer backgrounds which the wealthier take for granted.

Most of us intuit in our private lives that young people benefit greatly from somewhere to go, something to do and someone to talk to; that we have all learnt essential life skills from a responsible adult who knew more than us, a positive peer group, and access to a range of new opportunities.

---

68. For the avoidance of doubt, our point here is not about the 'rights' or 'wrongs' of private education, nor its impact (for good or ill) on society. Our value neutral point is simply that whether or not private schools succeed in conferring character and confidence on their young, this is typically what parents think they are buying through higher student: teacher ratios, greater resources and more extra-curricular activities. Parents are hoping to buy good youth work.

How do we know good youth work works?

In part because we've all been young once and it's not too tricky to remember what worked.[69]

Our point is not that youth work is the sole means of fostering capabilities, good character and strong society.

Our point is that our case for re-discovering youth work started out in sharp experience, has been affirmed by the rigour of science and endorsed by the proof of common sense.

So we believe some truths to be both proven and self-evident, namely that...

- Young people gain greatly from opportunities to come together and take responsibility

- We all need help at times in our life. And we all have something to give

- Finding the things you're good at and an adult who believes in you can change your life forever

69. Thanks to Craig Morley for this photo.

3. How youth work got forgotten

If our case is that youth work is a simple idea, and a good one, too often overlooked beyond the youth sector itself, how has it fallen from popular and political imagination?

Oscar Wilde once remarked of a spectacular Broadway flop that the play was a great success, the cast superb, but the audience, sadly, a disaster.

So is youth work's fading star:

a) symptomatic of declining standards in practice?

b) the consequence of poor communication? or

c) a function of the political class and public opinion's inability to watch and listen?

The quality of contemporary youth work

By virtue of young people choosing to be involved (or not, on any given sunny evening of the week), a relative degree of chaos is inherent in youth work.

However, it is also true that some youth work is under-planned and poorly delivered. As a whole, while subject to the usual monitoring requirements of specific funding streams, youth work as a whole has not benefited from the consistent application of quality standards. In the absence of clear standards, it has not been possible to distinguish on any consistent or transparent basis between charismatic leadership and true quality.

Further, good youth work requires both effective front-line provision and a strong organisation. Shaun Bailey, co-founder of *MyGeneration* in north Kensington and currently the Prime Minister's Special Advisor on Youth and Crime, talks about 'the business and the knitting circle', contrasting the community development feel and approach of a good youth worker with the straight lines and clean surfaces of a robust institution. Both are vital, yet too often, even where youth work is strong, organisation is less so.

A further operational hazard lies in the fact that good youth work is far from nine to five. As Gerry Glover of the iconic Bolton Girls' and Lads' Club says, 'if you want regular hours, forget it'. Clearly, this places demands on volunteers and paid staff alike. This, combined with the fact salary scales reward management more than delivery, has the effect of driving talented people away from the front-line as they enter their thirties, despite the fact their skill-set and strengths lie in face-to-face work with young people.

Our failure to articulate value

In late 2010, David Cameron's Youth Policy Advisor, Paul Oginsky, may have been brazen in blaming cuts to local youth services on youth workers' inability to articulate their value. Yet those most involved in youth work will privately concede the absence of compelling narrative emerging from within. To a degree, we have ourselves to criticise.

In part, our relative failure to speak truth to power and populace may be traced to an almost sectarian tendency...

• Voluntary sector youth workers are often not slow in their scorn for local authority employees

• Community youth organisations are frequently suspicious of large national agencies, perceived as parachuting in and hoovering up

• Uniformed and non-uniformed youth work can appear riven as opposed to simply distinctive

• Detached teams might not sit easily with centre-based colleagues

• Some see a fundamental schism between thematic and activity-based youth work; others still cleave exclusively to boys' or girls' work

Whilst an open examination of different approaches can, as in any sector, in theory, illuminate good practice, that isn't quite the same as arguing frantically on a pinhead, whilst alienating an interested but inexpert audience tiring of our squabbles.

A related snag is that some youth workers (in our honest view) do have a tendency to over-complicate and carve out narrow niches of expertise: if anyone can do it, how can we be special?

Historically, youth work has gone into print and speech to self-define as much by what it is not (teaching and probation) as by the good it can achieve.

A proliferation of national umbrella bodies (all undertaking valuable work in themselves) has possibly resulted in many voices eroding one clear message.

The cumulative effect of such self-inflicted brand degradation has not only been to try the patience of would-be supporters in policy and funding worlds. It has simultaneously driven many good programmes away from an association with youth work, thereby haemorrhaging good examples. For example, 'mentoring', 'youth leadership' and 'peer education' are just three titles taken by innumerable projects in the past decade attempting to escape the devalued yoke of 'youth work'. Now, as a result, youth work cannot call upon some of its strongest illustrations.

The focus of public attention

Youth work's fall from popular consciousness might be attributable to a number of inter-related cultural phenomena. As communities weaken[70] so, inevitably does a sense of collective responsibility for the development of young people. As the institutions, or pillars, of community have declined so have the 'natural' rallying points for youth. Technology, together with traffic and parental concern about public space has, it is suggested, resulted in young people spending less time in their communities.

---

70. Giddens (2006); Heywood (2008); Putnam (2000)

Equally corrosive, however, is the unintended consequence of societal triage. Here we return to Sam and Shafiq and the problem their respective stories sketch. Sam is on the wrong path and needs turning round. Shafiq is doing well and does not. Inevitably, Sam commands more concern than Shafiq.

The ramification, however, is that where youth work is referenced, it is increasingly through a narrative of remedy and redemption. In turn, casting youth work as a form of secular salvation pre-supposes that only young people at risk or in difficulty can benefit, where in fact the value of good youth work is universal. Everybody needs a good youth worker. And if youth work is something that only happens to disadvantaged young people at risk of offending, small wonder its popular appeal has declined. Youth work has become ghettoised.

Not only does this risk depriving the majority, it also alienates the principle of informal education from common understanding and wider application. For example, young people consistently tell us they want their teachers to have youth work skills (and that their best teachers already do). The fact youth work is increasingly seen through a problem-optic, however, is one reason why its skills are largely missing from the mainstream.

The limits of public policy

Investment in youth work is, in part, a casualty of public policy's inevitable yet limiting focus on specific problems.

For example, setting the outcome 'reducing knife carrying' sounds (and is) entirely logical. Yet often, the unintended consequence of programmes targeting a single issue is to constrain and contort interventions towards a particular, mechanical, linear and limited approach. As the section on the value of good youth work sets out, what may be of greater long-term value is investment in underlying capabilities and character. However, because public policy and funding need to hit quantifiable targets within time-bound horizons, there is a strong tendency to direct funding in more limited directions, targeting presenting symptoms not underlying causes.

In 2009, The Audit Commission concluded just this: that too many initiatives focused on pre-determined public policy targets and not on the complex reality of actual lives. In part, this is almost certainly an unintended consequence of the drive to greater accountability: the more funders seek specific results, and contracts crowd out grants, the more funds follow particular projects, almost certainly to the detriment of wider work building relationships with young people over the long-term. And it is almost certainly getting worse, as local authorities respond to central government budget cuts by ending provision of open access youth services, focusing solely on targeted support for those most in need.[71]

Again, on the face of it, this is understandable. But too great an emphasis on quantitative measures and pre-determined prescriptions leads to some weird, self-defeating dystopia in which on Monday night a young person is targeted as unemployed; on Tuesday another programme will work with the same individual to prevent an unplanned teenage pregnancy; and on Wednesday a third initiative will address the risk of knife carrying, without ever engaging with the individual and what's going on in their life as a whole.

Funding follows problems the state and media can box. In turn, organisations working with young people can become so driven to obsess as to whether a young person has been referred by the YOS or the YOT, to the YIP or the YISP, because they are NEET or in a PRU, to provide PAYP or IAG that at no point is space created to engage the young person standing in front of them. We need to not design the life out of work with young people.

71. Children and Young People Now (May 2011)

Inefficiencies in the funding economy

One youth organisation we know spent £249,000 last year. It has 27 different funding streams. Three of them last longer than 12 months. All have different reporting requirements.

Specifically, we identify four inter-related shortcomings of the status quo.[72]

1. Project-itis, meaning:

- Immediate outputs are prioritised over long-term impact

- Funding is insufficiently flexible to respond to changing circumstances

- Planning horizons are typically limited to one or three year cycles

- Key staff are not retained and core knowledge, competence and relationships are lost

- There is no incentive to outperform – excellence leads to increased service demand without a corresponding increase in resources, and/or funds are typically clawed back in the event of efficiency gains or leveraging of other income

2. Short-termism

Demands for unrealistic exit plans concoct the fiction that complex, deep-seated problems can be solved in arbitrary, fixed and short time frames. The result is frequently that faux-innovation is prioritised over the tried-and-tested and that delivery organisations are incentivised to over-claim.

---

72. Particular thanks to David Carrington for this summation.

3. Under-investment

Owing to this bias towards project funding over organisational capacity, and because project deliverables are still typically costed at a marginal or near marginal rate:

- There is insufficient investment in leadership, management and systems that ensure organisations run efficiently and effectively

- Organisations suffer capital starvation – lacking reserves for asset acquisition, working capital and development (including research and development and innovation)

4. High transaction costs

Multi-funding implies multiple applications and compliance with many monitoring processes.

All of this has and continues to undermine the important job of youth work.

4. What is to be done?

Honesty and quality

At London Youth, in 2007, we piloted a quality mark, built by colleagues at Hampshire Youth Options and designed specifically for open access, generic youth work. It measures and improves both how well an organisation is run and the quality of its youth work delivery, including the meaningful involvement of young people in decision-making and leadership. Thus far, 81 organisations have achieved the standard, with a further 65 working towards the first level (as of February 2013). All report that working through the scheme has improved front-line practice and institutional strength. In 2008, we began a partnership with City & Guilds to accredit the standard and assess awards (which also depends on young people's assessment). In early 2011, our own Trustee Board determined that by September 2013 full membership of London Youth would depend on achieving the Quality Mark.

Our reference, however, is not to lionise our own approach but rather underline the fundamental importance of introducing quality standards to youth work. Our overwhelming experience as a network of youth organisations across the capital is of a normal distribution of quality, ranging from outstanding to poor. Poor practice also undermines those delivering valuable work. As a movement, youth work needs to be brave about quality standards. So should funders.

Cross pollination

In our characterisation of good youth work, we were at pains to keep it both simple and broad. As such, we believe good youth work can take place in a wide variety of settings. Therefore, we argue that good youth work requires greater and higher-quality investment. Equally, we see room for importing youth work approaches to other contexts.

For example, the impact of delivering cognitive behavioural therapy in group settings in HM Young Offenders' Institution Portland as part of Positive Change illustrates the role the broad youth work approach can play within youth justice. Some staff in HMYOI Portland said taking part in the programme was a completely new, and clearly productive, way of working for them.

Conversely, for example, training for prison officers does not currently include conflict resolution. Importing youth work skills and approaches into the criminal justice system would appear both sensible and reasonably straightforward.

We have cited evidence that formal educational attainment in school is boosted significantly when teachers focus on wider personal and social development. We question whether orthodox school leadership and current teacher training makes this link with sufficient force and consistency. Is the notion that rounded education enhances formal educational attainment given sufficient airtime in schools? Certainly, the extension of the Academies programme and emergence of Free Schools should not be concerned 'only' with the acquisition of knowledge, but equally the capabilities to use it. Schools should also focus on the development of non-cognitive skills via youth work approaches – such as the introduction of extra-curricular activities into the existing or an extended school day, or the development of structured and sustained leadership opportunities for older students. If we can agree that the deliberate fostering of wider capabilities is important and that good youth work approaches are an effective means of achieving such, the central issue becomes how to deliver this in the most cost effective way. Developing partnerships and alliances between schools and youth clubs has to be one way of harnessing economies of scale.

UK Youth's Youth Achievement Foundations are demonstrating the success of taking a youth work approach to alternative curriculum provision for excluded pupils.

The example of our own previous work with Pimlico Plumbers and continued work with Wickes tradespeople illustrate the importance of bringing youth work's emphasis on capabilities and character into employment initiatives.

If we choose to make it so, the effects of good youth work can be incalculably diffusive.

Early intervention, adolescence and young adulthood

Early intervention has received much attention of late, acknowledging the crucial formative period of zero to three years.

We see, however, an emerging risk in public policy setting early years and adolescence in competition with one another – not least because in some quarters teenagers, who clearly do have a greater degree of self-determination than babies, might be seen as more 'deserving' of their 'fate' than small children, the more legitimate recipients of dwindling funds.

On closer inspection, however, setting early intervention and adolescence in a zero-sum game is wholly illogical.

First, given early intervention's focus on parenting and families, and the fact that many zero to three year olds in particular need are the children of young people, investing in late adolescence is also investing in early intervention: children born to teenage mothers are 63% more likely to live in poverty than children born to mothers in their twenties, and are themselves more likely to become teenage parents.[73]

Further, neurological research over the last ten years provides clear evidence of significant changes in both brain structure and function during adolescence. Whereas as IQ becomes largely stable by the age of ten, crucial non-cognitive skills remain particularly malleable during adolescence. Changes occur in teenage years particularly in areas relating to emotional balance, self-regulation, logical reasoning and executive functions such as planning, and are susceptible to environmental impact and intervention.[74]

We are absolutely not arguing against the emphasis on early intervention, simply that we should not fall into the trap of either, or.

---

73. Mayhew and Bradshaw (2005)
74. Steinberg (2009); Heckman (2011)

We also see a need for greater attention to be given to the 16 to 25 age range. Our experience is that in this transition from adolescence, young people move rapidly from specialist structures and support to mainstream adult provision. Be this in education, employment, housing, health or criminal justice, there appears to be something of a public policy blind spot relating to young adulthood.

Targeted and open-access

We argue, on the basis of evidence and observation, that public funding should be increased for broad-based personal and social development programmes.

In the current economic climate it is difficult to argue against the fact that money must be focused on greatest need and those young people at risk.

It is also true that social class is still the strongest single predictor of formal educational attainment.[75] So it is also not unreasonable to suggest that youth work and what it can achieve with and for young people is of even greater importance in poorer communities.

However, our argument for the re-prioritisation of character and value of youth work looks not, ultimately, to the shelf-life of the current spending round, nor to certain sections of society, but to a generation of policy-making and the whole of national life. As such, in the long view, we are wary of over-targeting.

Foremost, evidence and experience demonstrate that every one of us depends in later life on our personal qualities and social competence.

We have also set out the risk of seeing youth work solely as a remedial activity.

75. Norris (July 2011)

Furthermore, the distinction between targeted and open-access services, in effect, is not clean and simple. We ourselves see (working directly with 21,000 young people a year) that open access services (that young people choose to engage with) are often the way in which disadvantaged and at risk young people access support initially: community based-youth work in particular can be not only a highly effective but also, for some young people, either the only positive engagement and/or the critical access route to specialised support.

Openly accessible services are also, by definition, powerful means of bringing young people from different backgrounds and perspectives together. (Three out of five young people reported that youth work had helped them better understand people who are different from themselves.)[76] Social mixing should be a key policy objective and youth work can play a powerful role.

Without doubt, as our broad definition and subsequent taxonomy set out, specific objectives for particular groups of young people require differing forms of intervention. Yet the common sense of targeting resources and methods appropriately should not, over the long-term, crowd out deliberate and sustained investment in bringing young people together and developing every young person's competence and character.

Intelligent assessment

In our day-to-day work we are often disappointed by the polarisation of debate on how best to assess what works.

We see an unhelpful, binary division between the evidence fundamentalists and measurement deniers: we meet some front-line workers who, in our view, are overly sceptical as to the value of impact assessment; and we meet a number of funders and research agencies who seem to under-estimate the cost and limitations of reliable evaluation.

---

76. Merton et al. (2004)

We feel the following might represent practical improvements to the status quo:

- Greater focus should be given to the honest difficulty of time-lag (between the point at which an intervention is made and its outcome); and to the challenge of proving a negative. (Did a young person not offend because of youth work?) Because the world is complicated and impacts young people in many different ways, it is near enough impossible to isolate single factors. So, when assessing the causal relationship between intervention and outcome, we should shift the burden of proof from attribution (demanding an intervention proves it has alone affected an outcome) to contribution ('what we did to play a part').

- There is a real risk that funding begins to follow not, in fact, the most effective work but organisations best placed to tell their story (albeit on the basis of social science not bid-writing). There is no automatic correlation between an organisation's ability to pay for and develop sufficient research expertise and the quality of their front-line youth work. The skill-set required to design and conduct rigorous research is not the same as that required to engage effectively with young people. This potentially disadvantages small voluntary youth organisations with limited staff and resources who are often the most effective at reaching the most disengaged young people. It also risks a disproportionate diversion of scarce resource from front-line delivery.

- We see enormous potential for the closer working between the statutory, voluntary and academic sectors, based on each sector's strengths. Through on-the-ground youth programmes, social researchers can gain access to research participants in real-life settings; youth agencies can benefit from academic research expertise to evaluate their work; and genuine public service innovation can result from rigorously evidenced conclusions. In particular, we call for sensible investment in high-quality longitudinal research.

Research in epidemiology, for example, highlights the importance of longitudinal studies to understand the detailed, causal relationships between complex and inter-related social factors and health outcomes. We see a clear comparative case for understanding informal education.

- The Greater London Authority's Project Oracle represents a great step forward. Here the aim has been to establish a meta-architecture, a set of standards against which different forms of evidence can be set. At a stroke this moves debate on from competition between differing tools (such as social audit, social return on investment or subjective well-being questionnaires), focusing instead on verifying the reliability of varying claims. We would strongly suggest that the establishment of top-level standards is a more valuable way ahead than an attempt to determine top-down which assessment tool should be used – not least as many charities have invested considerable time and money in different methodologies.

- Similarly, the outcomes framework from The Young Foundation (2012) is another significant advance, helping to standardise the evidence base and make impact assessment more accessible to practitioners.

- It is indubitably true that what gets measured gets managed. So we welcome the national well-being project from the Office of National Statistics as an early attempt to re-balance the books with investigation into fulfilment alongside econometrics. We look forward to finding nationally agreed ways of measuring young people's development beyond exams and tests of cognitive abilities (important though they are).

Finally, we also call (a little in the manner of filing a minority report) for calm consideration of a parallel approach to assuring impact. For the avoidance of doubt we are, emphatically, in favour of understanding impact.

Yet in place of requiring every programme to assess impact uniquely, every funded initiative might instead be required to demonstrate that it:

(a) Has a clear logic model – of what it is trying to achieve and how; and

(b) Quality assures its deliverable

This might be a more practical and proportionate approach that would achieve three things:

- One, it would ensure that in each programme there is a clear structure for personal and social development (as opposed merely to a cornucopia of ill-thought-through activities)

- Two, it would establish clearly the intended impact and method of any given programme, thereby enabling a ready gauge of likely effectiveness by cross-referencing with extant research from pre-existing initiatives

- Three, the insistence on quality assurance would improve practical delivery and establish a reasonable working proxy for impact

This simple, two-part formula (logic model plus quality assurance) could then be supplemented at a global level by very high quality, longitudinal studies of manageable cohorts derived from sample initiatives, mitigating the costs and risks of universal impact assessment. For currently the quantity of monitoring and evaluation data captured does seem to undermine quality: the more data captured the less it is verified, assessed and unpicked.

As such and in short, we wonder if assessing impact must always, in every project, be the only or optimal way of assuring it.

Intelligent funding

A lack of access to capital along with overly restricted, short-term grants and contracts act as a barrier to youth organisations achieving their social mission. The pitfall of over-reliance upon short-life, project-focused grants has been established beyond debate.

The principles of redress are relatively straightforward. They centre on recognising the working capital requirements of civil society organisations, proportionate reporting, sensible timescales and the need to build strong institutions through strategic investment. They are well set out by others elsewhere.[77]

Smart commissioning

In commissioning, as great a value should be placed on work begetting intrinsic outcomes (related to underlying capabilities) and promoting protective factors (such as resilience, social skills and a pro-social peer group) – as it is on projects focused on extrinsic value (such as increasing employability and reducing crime) and specific risks (such as truancy and teen pregnancy).

We suggest that the relative ease of assessing extrinsic and risk factors creates an unreliable optic; it privileges that which is more readily measurable over work which may, in the long-run, be more profound in its consequences. Hard evidence has established beyond reasonable doubt that investing in intrinsic value and protective factors mitigates the threat of specific risk factors (such as truancy and anti-social behaviour), and creates extrinsic value (such as increasing employment and reducing offending).[78]

---

77. In particular see the work of Clara Miller, President of The Nonprofit Finance Fund in New York and especially *The Looking-Glass World of Nonprofit Money*; www.venturesome.org.uk; Unwin (2003); Report of The NCVO Funding Commission (2010)

78. Reschly et al. (2008); Bernat et al. (2006); Scwartz et al. (2010); Lerner et al. (2009)

For example, in their concluding report of March 2011, the London Serious Youth Violence Board identified the role of risk factors contributing to unemployment and its associated lack of financial security, leading to an increase in crime. In so doing it went on to emphasise the role of protective factors, as counterbalancing forces. It highlighted the importance of holistic approaches, engaging and developing the whole young person and working with local organisations who have built trust in neighbourhoods over the long-term. In other words, tackling a presenting symptom requires underlying work on protective factors and intrinsic value.

Understanding, and backing, the relationship between intrinsic and extrinsic value, and between risk and protective factors, will be absolutely critical in creating long-term taxpayer value. This should be a hallmark of intelligent commissioning, especially in light of payment by results.

The challenge of investing in capabilities and character, as opposed to presenting symptoms, however, is not confined to the public purse. Independent trusts and foundations, and corporate social responsibility programmes, could equally invest in underlying capabilities as well as more instrumental interventions geared towards specific deficits.

Confident politics

The investment case for rounded individuals stands on firm economic and scientific ground. We also claim personal experience and the proof of common human sense.

So imagine the Prime Minister explaining on the Today programme that, no, she appreciated that the £billion investment just made in informal education, in broad-based personal and social development did not focus exclusively on specific problems. But, mindful of the known costs of crime, unemployment and family breakdown and noting evidence and experience alike, her government knew that ensuring all young people learn from a trusted adult, a positive peer group and a range of opportunities would yield clear gains for individuals and society alike. Making certain that every young person can access good examples, structured fun and the chance to take responsibility was bound to build the capabilities and character of young Britons, to the life-long good of the realm. This investment (the Prime Minister might conclude) was based on much more than a hunch.

Good youth work is a simple idea of both proven and intuitive value. A degree of transference from universal experience, underlying science and personal logic to politics and public policy could move us leaps and bounds.

We all know underlying capabilities are important. They are underplayed in public policy only because they are hard to crystallise and difficult to quantify.

So we call for new confidence in public policy and greater character in our politics.

In part, our plea is a question of leadership.

End note

When Stelios Haji-Ioannou discovered that the only way to run flights on the Geneva-Barcelona route was to sell a package that included accommodation, he bought five tents from a discount store (price £19.99 each) and erected them on a campsite outside Barcelona.

Sometimes, pressing problems need oblique strategies. Tackling youth unemployment, crime, violence, fragmenting families and divided communities – finding joy in art, sport, nature and neighbourhood may owe more to lateral development than overt instrumentalism.

In 1953, W. McG. Eager, tracing the history of 'boys' clubs and related movements' opened his account by noting that:

"The 19th century was well advanced; the too-solid foundations of Victorian respectability were cracking; the complacency and cocksureness of the Palmerstonian era were being shivered by rumbling vibrations of doubt and dissatisfaction, before either thinkers or men and women of action noted that society comprised not only adults and children, but also adolescent boys and girls. They discerned an intermediate age, plastic, impressionable, perilous and formative. They took action independently and spontaneously".

And so, at the dawn of the old century, you could scarcely move, it must have felt, without finding a new institution built for, with and by young people – the scouts, girls' clubs, the flowering of the settlements to name but a few – all emphasising self-government and civic care.

So if, historically, strife has begat strides forward, when this downturn turns up, then, if not before, we need another adolescent spring – a new enlightenment of youth, in which we place confidence less in targets and initiatives and more in character and the reason of rounded individuals.

It need not be hard. It could be profound. It will require rigorous delivery, intelligent metrics, public hope and political courage. Most of all it requires us all, as urged in another austerity Britain, in a speech in 1949:

"...to see ourselves, not as isolated practitioners of particular techniques in adolescent education, but as a movement of vision and determination, a movement of joy and friendship and laughter, a movement that is helping to set going a yet mightier movement of the human spirit, which may bring out of this age of doubts and difficulties, a revitalising of our nation and our soul".[79]

79. Hubert Secretan OBE, to the 24th annual conference of the National Association of Boys' Clubs, Leeds, July 1949

Summary of the argument

London Youth's Positive Change Programme engaged young people involved in youth violence and gang culture and supported them into education, employment and training. As Positive Change was evaluated, however, learning became less clearly tied to specific interventions tackling particular problems and increasingly woven with a wider (and brighter) fabric that spoke of increasing character and capabilities, knowledge and networks.

Positive Change highlighted the importance of developing rounded individuals by building relationships between young people and trusted adults, developing a positive peer group and creating a range of new opportunities.

Our experience is corroborated by all the available evidence across economics, psychology and neuroscience pointing to the importance of non-cognitive skills and capabilities in order to achieve a range of positive outcomes as young people transition from adolescence to adulthood. Such skills are becoming increasingly important, as pathways from compulsory education to the workplace and 'adult society' become more varied and complex.

As such, we argue that public policy and funding should focus less on presenting symptoms and more on developing young people's underlying competence. Too often funding follows problems the state can box. The key question for funders, policy makers and everybody who is interested in the promotion of a strong society should be: how do we develop capabilities and character?

Good youth work is a significant part of the answer. Public and philanthropic funding should be increased for broad-based personal and social development. Good youth work (which we define broadly and which is structured and goes well beyond the simple provision of leisure activities) has a proven positive impact on personal and social development.

Youth work is no silver bullet. Young people grow up amidst myriad influences. We also acknowledge the limitations of the evidence base for youth work. Yet the cumulative effect of evaluations of individual programmes, anecdotal evidence and a plethora of studies connecting youth work with educational attainment, increased employability, the prevention of offending and wider life-skills passes the test of any reasonable person.

The efficacy of good youth work is intuitive as well as proven. We have all been young and can remember what worked. We can all recall inspiring adult role models, learning with our peers outside the classroom and the importance of feeling part of something, proud of something. And the chance to find the things we're good at. There's more to all of us than we think, and good youth work helps draw that out.

But youth work has been forgotten and fallen out of mainstream popular, political and media debate. We suspect a number of possible reasons including: variable quality; the inability of youth workers to articulate the value of what they do; and inefficiencies in the funding economy and public policy that incentivise youth organisations to focus on fixed-term projects and short-run outputs at the expense of long-term trust and lasting impact.

So we offer a vision for youth in post-austerity Britain that invests hard in the capabilities and character of the next generation.

To bring this vision to life we need to invest in youth work and develop youth work approaches in parallel fields (such as teaching). We must broaden our notion of a good education to include capabilities and character as well as the acquisition of skills and knowledge.

In turn, we need to find ways of robust, consistent and proportionate assessment of the efficacy of youth work. We need to be assertive about quality assurance. We require an intelligent funding and commissioning landscape acknowledging real change is made by strengthening communities and individuals over the long-term. And, perhaps, most importantly, we need brave leadership that not only understands the value of capabilities and character, but actively sets about prioritising it.

About the author

London Youth is a network of over 400 diverse community youth organisations where young people choose to go. Somewhere near you, there's one of our members, at work every day and most nights – plus over 399 others in neighbourhoods across the capital.

We grew from the Ragged Schools movement in the 1880s, spending the 20th Century as the Union of Youth Clubs and Federation of Boys' Clubs. Throughout, our mission has been to support and challenge young people to become the best they can be.

Our vision is that all young Londoners access a wide range of high quality opportunities for learning and fun, beyond family and formal education, building strong trusted relationships with adults and their peers; leading to raised aspirations, broadened networks and increased confidence, character and skills. Today, we try and achieve this in three ways.

Development

We help our member organisations increase their effectiveness by training youth workers, providing information and supporting organisations to achieve the London Youth Quality Mark (accredited by City & Guilds).

Opportunity

We work directly with young people, innovating and delivering programmes with and through our network, creating a broad range of opportunities that a single community-based organisation working alone could not. (We do this through programmes focused on sport, youth leadership, employability, outdoor education and other creative approaches, in London and out of town at our two residential learning centres.)

Voice

And we ensure our expertise and the on-the-ground voices of youth workers and young people influence public policy, practice and opinion. (Hence *Hunch*.)

References

Please visit our website for the full bibliography.

Acknowledgements

This work has been produced by hundreds of heads. We are enormously grateful to everybody whose practice has inspired and whose ideas have illuminated.

Any errors, omissions or oddities are owing to poor translation and entirely the fault of London Youth.

We are particularly grateful to Lord Victor Adebowale for chairing the Positive Change programme board and encouraging us into print. Victor was joined on the board by James Cleverly, Dinar Hossain, Baroness Shireen Ritchie, Graham Robb, Claire Belgard and Brendan O'Keefe – busy people all who gave their time and ideas generously and to whom we are very grateful. Emma Morris delivered cognitive behavioural therapy in HMYOI Portland. Bryan Merton emphasised the value of getting people talking. Geoff Mulgan reminded us about Oliver Wendell Holmes and Oscar Wilde. General the Lord Guthrie encouraged us to see that youth work is a universal idea. Jamie Audsley, Mark Griffiths, Helen Hibbert, Charlotte Hill, Gaynor Humphreys, Mat Ilic, Bethia McNeil, Adam Nichols, Matthew Taylor and Ashley Whittaker were invaluable first readers to whom we are indebted. Kyle Baker, Shaun Bailey, Simon Blake, Sir Stuart Etherington, Winston Goode, Thomas Lawson, Susanne Rauprich and Curtis Watson also helped shaped our argument. Of the texts that underpin our discourse we were particularly struck by *Freedom's Orphans* from the IPPR, Demos' *Character Inquiry* and *Grit* by The Young Foundation. Tim Saunders, Clive Winter and Katie Worthington are three of the many youth workers in our network to whom we regularly turn for insight and perspective. Terry Birch, David Cornock-Taylor, Doug Pratt and David Hatchard continue to be expert witnesses as to what life was like growing up in a youth club in the mid twentieth century. Thank you all.[80]

---

80. Rosie Ferguson, Maymay Knight, Shivangee Patel and Nick Wilkie respectively would also like to thank Sally Abbott, Dolores Lee, Caroline Dunton and Michael de Weymarn, without whom…

I would not give a fig for the simplicity this side of complexity.
I would give my life for the simplicity on the other side of complexity.

Oliver Wendell Homes Jnr.

Never invest in any idea you can't illustrate with a crayon.

Peter Lynch